BEI GRIN MACHT SICH IHR WISSEN BEZAHLT

- Wir veröffentlichen Ihre Hausarbeit, Bachelor- und Masterarbeit

- Ihr eigenes eBook und Buch - weltweit in allen wichtigen Shops

- Verdienen Sie an jedem Verkauf

Jetzt bei www.GRIN.com hochladen und kostenlos publizieren

Jutta Mahlke

Britische Kolonialgeschichte im Unterricht. Indiens Unabhängigkeit in Salman Rushdies fiktionalem Textauszug "Methwold's Game"

GRIN Verlag

Bibliografische Information der Deutschen Nationalbibliothek:

Die Deutsche Bibliothek verzeichnet diese Publikation in der Deutschen National-
bibliografie; detaillierte bibliografische Daten sind im Internet über http://dnb.d-
nb.de/ abrufbar.

Impressum:

Copyright © 2008 GRIN Verlag GmbH
Druck und Bindung: Books on Demand GmbH, Norderstedt Germany
ISBN: 978-3-640-22751-8

LK 12

Unterrichtsentwurf im Fach Englisch

Thema der Unterrichtsreihe:

The Postcolonial Experience in India

Thema der Unterrichtsstunde:

Indiens Unabhängigkeit als Wendepunkt britischer Kolonialgeschichte dargestellt in Salman Rushdie's fiktionalem Textauszug „*Methwold's Game*" (aus: *Midnight's Children*)

1. Geplanter Verlauf der Unterrichtsreihe

Einheit (Std.)	Thema: Sequenz und Einheit
Lead-In (2 Std.)	*Advance Organizer: Timeline (Postcolonialism) of the British Empire*
1. (2 Std.)	1) H. Kureishi's fiktionaler Textauszug "Clash of Cultures" (aus "Buddha of Suburbia") 2) The Commonwealth of Nations
2. (4 Std.)	1) **Webquest Postcolonialism in India** – Komplexe Themen- und aufgabenorientierte Internetrecherche zur Vorbereitung von Präsentationen zu sechs thematischen Schwerpunkten (*Gandhi's principles, Nehru, India within the Commonwealth of Nations, women, caste system, Indian Press* und *Bollywood*) des postkolonialen Indien 2) Autoren britisch-indischer postkolonialer Literatur (Salman Rushdie als indisch-britischer Schriftsteller postkolonialer indischer Literatur in englischer Sprache, Hanif Kureishi als Schriftsteller der Literatur der "*Indian Minorities in Britain*")
3. (2 Std.) hier wären 4 Stunden möglich (Doppelstunden: Speeches, fiktionale Texte)	**Die Bedeutung von Indien's Unabhängigkeit in politischer Rede und fiktionalem Text** 1) Politische Reden im kolonialen (Macaulay's Minute on Education, 1835) und unabhängigen Indien (Nehru's Tryst with Destiny, 1947) 2) **Salman Rushdie's fiktionaler Textauszug „Methwold's Game" (aus: Midnight's Children)**
4. (2 Std.)	India – The Postcolonial Experience – Teampräsentationen (Teil 1+2)
5. (2 Std.)	India – The Postcolonial Experience – Teampräsentationen (Teil 3)
6. (2 Std.)	Fiktionaler Text 3
	Exam/Test

2. Ziele der Unterrichtsstunde

2.1 Übergeordnetes Lernziel

Die SuS sollen ...

den Text multiperspektivisch in kooperativer Gruppenarbeit bearbeiten können, indem sie aufgabenorientiert auf Vorwissen zurückgreifen, um den ausgewählten literarischen Text der Textsorte angemessen zu analysieren und im historischen Kontext mit seiner Gegenwartsbedeutung darzustellen.

2.2 Wesentliche Teillernziele

2.2.1 Kognitive Lernziele

Die SuS sollen

- ... Informationen aus dem literarischen Textauszug *„Methwold's Game"* von Salman Rushdie nach verschiedenen Verarbeitungsinteressen (Detailverstehen, Analyse, Stellungnahme aufgrund von Textkriterien) gezielt aufnehmen (selektieren) können.
- ... aus dem literarischen Textauszug *„Methwold's Game"* von Salman Rushdie Aussagen aus Textzusammenhang und individuellem Vorwissen mit Hinweisen auf stilistische Mittel selbstständig erschließen (inferieren) können
- ... das Gelesene weiterdenken, um begründet auf dieser fiktionalen postkolonialen Literatur (nicht nur, sondern integriert in Faktenwissen!) zum Thema Stellung nehmen zu können (elaborieren).

2.2.2 Sozial – affektives Lernziel

Die SuS sollen ...

- kooperative Arbeitsformen für die Textarbeit zunehmend eigenverantwortlich und selbstbestimmt nutzen können.
- sich auf neuartige postkoloniale Literatur einlassen können. (interkulturelles Lernen)

3. Hausaufgaben

3.1 Hausaufgaben zur Stunde:

➢ *Reading task "Methwold's Game" since 10.11. for today: prepare - use study aids – choose 2 tasks out of study aids 4) to 9)! (Text 4, S. 14 ff., schriftlich)*[1]

3.2 Hausaufgaben der Stunde:

➢ *Try to define postcolonial literature and continue work on your presentations. Keep both texts in mind, Kureishi's Buddha of Suburbia and Rushdie's Midnight's Children. Their perspectives and devices are the same genre but differ greatly in style.*

---

[1] ***Erwartungshorizont für die Hausaufgabe: Comprehension***

4) Countdown until Independence of India: 1st (ll. 1 – 107): 70 days until independence: Indians buy the Estates even though they alienate them (pictures, habits ...) 2nd (ll. 108 – 146): 30 days/complaints on the phone; budgies, goldfish, cat is terrified by the dogs, fear: fan will slice off head in the night, pianola (great fun!), cocktail cabinet 3rd (ll. 146 – 158 (end)): 20 days – transition: Methwold's Estate is changing them: Oxford drawl, enjoy cocktail hour – Sabkuch ticktock hai/All is well. (Development: Fine British Indians by the time Independence comes - The former master – owner of Estate/sahib – Mr. Methwold, uses an Indian slogan, which he repeats three times, to make them feel more comfortable while they slip into an Oxford drawl, whenever he appears!) Language learning (and cultural) awareness – transition – or ill country ?(Nehru)

5) selling it cheeply to „suitable persons" who agree on his two conditions, to buy complete with all contents without changes or throwing away and to take over at the exact moment of Indian Independence – an allegory to 1633 Methwold's trade with the West, his vision becoming the city of Bombay, the purchasers Amina and Ahmed Sinai becoming the narrator's parents, who himself will be a Midnight's child, born in Bombay at midnight August 14, 1947. Saleem is one of 1001 children born at the stroke of midnight, named Midnight's children. 70 days before Independence they probably knew that they expected a child around that time and therefore looked for the houses (ll.71-81). That's how the story goes. That was Methwold's allegorical game (l. 51) in the story. (S. Rushdie was also born in Bombay in 1947 just before Independence, an almost, but not a real Midnight's child which is an allegory to India (she, the nation) being independendent and born or reborn.) Rushdie is muslim so one can even draw a parallel to the newly founded Pakistan as a new-born nation and allegory but knowing about the whole plot, India is the important history, it really is India he writes about!

6) advantages: price, not much more! Amid discovers the „delights of fine Scotch whisky" (l.135 f.), celebrate cocktail hour, sharp edges get blurred (l.147 f.), learn about ceiling fans, gas cookers, imitate Oxford drawl; disadvantages: afraid of ceiling fans, hate dogs, goldfish, paint, full cupboards, living out of suitcases, no room for suits, live like Britishers, no water, only toilet paper! British pictures, drinking is not good, ...

7) Buckingham Villa (Mr. Methwold's), Versailles Villa, Sans Souci, ... Imperial names; not just British, even more pomp!

8)They discover the Pianola and Scotch whisky. They believe Mr. Methwold is eccentric and drains his glass at one go.

9) Mr. Methwold seems happy: He mumbles „All is well" in Hindustani: Sabkuch ticktock hai!

4. Geplanter Verlauf der Unterrichtsstunde

Unterrichtsphase	Sach- und Verhaltensaspekte	Arbeits- und Sozialform	Medien
Einstieg ►Aufgreifen von Vorwissen d. Vorstunde und erarbeitende Hausaufgaben 5-10 min	SuS tragen die Lösungen 4) – 9) vor und ergänzen ggfs.. Kurzes L.- Feedback.[2]	Frontal UG	Hefte Textbook S. 13-16 S. 16, 4-9
Hinführung ►Problematisierung der Analyse und Stellungnahme zum Text 5 min	L erteilt Arbeitsauftrag: Analyze the text and comment on both based on Methwold's Game: *India (Aug 15 – 1947) Decolonization or Independence? Use 17: What are the advantages of this kind of fictional view (...)?.* Write a placemat![3] SuS formulieren den Auftrag mit eigenen Worten	Frontal	Placemats der Vorstunde (leere Extras) S. 15, 16, 10- 14, 15-18, insb. „Allegory" und 17
Erarbeitung ►THINK ►SQUARE 15 min	SuS bearbeiten einzeln arbeitsteilig den Opinion Auftrag India (Aug 15 – 1947) Decolonization <u>or</u> Independence ? SuS beschriften (die Rückseiten der zur Unabhängigkeit Indien anhand der Rede gefertigten) placemats SuS tauschen sich durch Lesen und Kommentare gruppenweise aus	EA GA	Placemats
Sicherung ►**SHARE** und Feedback 15 min	SuS tauschen sich im Kurs miteinander aus. SUS und L. Feedback. SuS geben abschließenden Kommentar eines Experten jeder Gruppe. (evtl. L. Feedback)	*Galleriegang* *1 Stay, 3 Stray* Blitzlichtrunde[4]	
Hausaufgabe	Vgl. 3.2		

---

[2] Planvariante: SuS kontrollieren und überarbeiten die Hausaufgaben (Hefte austauschen bearb. 4) bis 9) gegenseitig beantworten!)

[3] *Ergänzung zum L-Auftrag: flip to the other side! (or use new one if not readable otherwise!) Think (5 min.), Square (10 min.), Share – 1 Stay – 3 Stray (10 min)! You are welcome to use your additional material, see p. 15 and of previous lessons and study aids.*

[4] Planvarianten: Kann je nach Situation entfallen oder anstelle des Galleriegangs bis zur Teampräsentation ausgeweitet werden

5. Didaktisch – methodischer Kommentar

5.1 Sachstruktureller Entwicklungsstand der Lerngruppe

Anhand der historischen Zeitleiste, des Zitat's „*The Empire writes back (to the center)*" (S. Rushdie) und eines ersten fiktionalen Texts wurde ein literaturtheoretischer Ansatz vorbereitet, der englische Texte aus den ehemaligen Kolonialgebieten (Rushdie) ebenso wie die neuere Migrantenliteratur Großbritanniens (Kureishi) umfasst, die unter *East* das ehemalige Indien (*East Asia*: Indien, Pakistan und Bangladesh) und *West* das Abendland, insbesondere das *mothercountry* Großbritannien verstehen. Anhand zweier politischer Reden, Macaulay's „*Minute on Indian Education*" (1835) und Nehru's „*Tryst with Destiny*" (1947) zur Staatsgründung des neuen demokratischen unabhängigen Indien haben sich die SUS auch mit dem sprachpolitischen Rahmen der Kolonialisierung in Indien beschäftigt und der Sprache als Machtinstrument der herrschenden Klassen zur Kolonialzeit Großbritanniens. In „*Clash of Cultures*" (H. Kureishi), der die Rolle junger Frauen und den Generationskonflikt der patriarchalischen Elterngeneration in Migrantenfamilien mit deren Kindern als „Jugendliche zwischen zwei Welten" und „*arranged marriages*" diskutiert, wurde die laxe Moral des Westens als Konfliktpotential herausgestellt. Zur Person Rushdies bemerkte ein Schüler, dass Rushdie scheinbar eine Haltung wie Gandhi einnehmen wolle. Vermutungen wie diese sollen nun anhand des Textes konkretisiert und insbesondere dem allegorischen Inhalt begegnet werden. Sollte bereits der antizipierte Leser in der postkolonialen Literatur als wesentliches Stilmerkmal, durch das sich Rushdie und Kureishi im Detail unterscheiden, erkannt werden, übertrifft das die Erwartungen dieser Stunde.

5.2 Anbindung an den Lehrplan

Kommunikative Fähigkeiten und Fertigkeiten zur literarischen Textrezeption und die multiperspektivische Bearbeitung komplexer Aufgabenstellungen solen an diesen postkolonialen fiktionalen Textauszügen möglichst schüler- und wissenschaftsorientiert geschult werden. Sie stellen einen Schwerpunkt für das Zentralabitur 2010 dar.

5.3 Didaktisch – methodische Überlegungen

Rezipationsästhetischer (top down) und rezipientenorientierte (bottom up) Zugänge sollen schüleraktivierende Begegnung mit postkolonialer Literatur ermöglichen, die einen mehrfachen Perspektivwechsel der SuS erfordern. Fiktionale Textauszüge ausgewählter Autoren des Viewfinder „*The Postcolonial Experience*" sind eingebettet in die Unabhängigkeit Indiens im *Commonwealth of Nations*. Methodisch sind kooperative Verfahren (Placemat) und Rückgriff auf Vorwissen zur Textarbeit vorgesehen.

<u>**6. Literaturliste**</u>

- Ashcroft, Bill et. al. *"The Empire writes back – theory and practice in postcolonial literatures"*, Routledge, 2005
- Butzko, Ellen: Klett Workshop: The Clash of Cultures in a globalized World (Teilnahme in der Lehrerfortbildung mit Schwerpunkt *African Perspective*, Reader), 2006
- Sabine Doff, Friederike Klippel: Englisch Didaktik, Praxishandbuch für die Sekundarstufe I und II, Cornelsen, 2008
- Haß, Frank (Hrsg.) Fachdidaktik Englisch, Ernst Klett Verlag GmbH, Stuttgart, 2006
- Hinz, Klaus: Kognitiv-analytisch und affektiv-kreativ gesteuerte Aktivitäten im fremdsprachlichen Literaturunterricht – ein Unterrichtsmodell für das Fach Englisch in: PRAXIS 47 (2000) 3, S. 235 ff.
- MSSWF: Sekundarstufe I. Gymnasium Englisch. Kernlehrplan (G8), 2007
- MSSWF: Richtlinien und Lehrpläne für das Gymnasium - Sekundarstufe II - in Nordrhein-Westfalen – Englisch, unveränderter Nachdruck, 2003
- Salman Rushdie: *„Methworld's Game"* in: Mitchell, Michael: *The Postcolonial Experience – Decolonizing the Mind*, Viewfinder Topics, Langenscheidt, 2005, S. 13 ff.
- http://www.langenscheidt.de/katalog/linkfinder-rb-11.html
- www.postcolonialweb.org
- *http://www.davidcrystal.com/*

<u>7. Anhang</u>

- http://homepage.ruhr-uni-bochum.de/Jutta.Mahlke/html/lk_12_-_webquest.html (selbst erstellter Webquest, durch Handout individuell ergänzen, Langenscheidt Links zu Topics Viewfinder können direkt verlinkt werden!)
- Handout zum Webquest (zur Vorbereitung von Schülerteampräsentationen)
- Mögliche vereinbarte Agenda zur Unterrichtsreihe
- *Speeches* (T.B. Macaulay, 1835, Nehru, 1947, in der Schülerversion einseitig mit Zeilennummern versehen) und Skizze mit Placemat (Thema Vorgabe) der Vorstunde

(anpassen für Kurs – Aufgaben zum Text etc. sinnvoll!)

India (Aug 15-1947)

Decolonization <u>or</u> Independence?

<u>**Skizze 1. Stunde**</u>

Unterrichtsphase	*Sach- und Verhaltensaspekte*	*Arbeits- und Sozialform*	*Medien*
Einstieg ►informierender Einstieg (gist) ►Advance Organizer 10 min	• S. (T.-B. M.) hält die Rede (Member of Parliament, East India Company and Indian Committee). SuS stellen Situation 1835 dar. • SuS lesen die wesentlichen Teile der Rede nach. • Wortschatz und Bedeutung klären: Kontext[5]	Frontal Historisches Roleplay I	Rede T.B. Macaulay: „Minute on Indian Education" (1835)
Hinführung ► durch Problematisierung 5 min	➤ Stimmungsbild – Abstimmung (nach ersten Abschnitten der Rede möglich!) ➤ SuS diskutieren erarbeiten Leitfragen zur Diskussion der Sprachenfrage im kolonialen Indien. (L. berät)	Podiums-diskussion	Tafel
Erarbeitung ►Information zur Methode Placemat ►durch Bearbeitung der Aufgabe ►THINK (Konstruktion) ►SQUARE (Ko-Konstruktion)	• L-Impuls: India's Independence! SuS nennen das Datum und antizipieren den Redner! S (Nehru) trägt seine Unabhängigkeitsrede vor. (gist) (SuS stellen die indische Versammlung in Neu Delhi zur Feierstunde dar.) 2. Vortrag SuS lesen mit. (detail) L erteilt Auftrag zum Fertigen der Placemats: Impuls: Use background information and Nehru's speech: language, title, stylistic devices • Titel: India on Aug. 15, 1947 - Decolonization or Independence? • SuS beschriften einzeln Placemats. • SuS fertigen gruppenweise Placemats • SuS lesen und ergänzen die Placemats.	Frontal Historisches Rollenspiel 2 EA GA	Tafel 4 placemats
Sicherung **5-10 min** ►SHARE	➤ Placemats werden ausgetauscht (1 stay – 3 stray). L. gibt Feedback. ➤ Placemats werden ausgestellt (Gallerie)	Galleriegang (1 stay – 3 stray) (Pause)	

---

[5] L. Impulse: mögl. bereits recherchierte SuS-Antworten: 1833 Slavery in British Empire abolished! 1837 – 1901 Queen Victoria – Victorian Age – British Empire extends! (Sprachenpolitik, Bildung in der Kolonie – Macht, Demokratie, geschichtliche Bedeutung?)

On Indian Education[6]

We now come to the gist of the matter. We have a fund to be employed as Government shall direct for the intellectual improvement of the people of this country. The simple question is, what is the most useful way of employing it?

All parties seem to be agreed on one point, that the dialects commonly spoken among the natives of this part of India, contain neither literary nor scientific information, and are, moreover, so poor and rude that, until they are enriched from some other quarter, it will not be easy to translate any valuable work into them. It seems to be admitted on all sides, that the intellectual improvement of those classes of the people who have the means of pursuing higher studies can at present be effected only by means of some language not vernacular amongst them.

What then shall that language be? One-half of the Committee maintain that it should be the English. The other half strongly recommend the Arabic and Sanscrit. The whole question seems to me to be, which language is the best worth knowing?

I have no knowledge of either Sanscrit or Arabic.-But I have done what I could to form a correct estimate of their value. I have read translations of the most celebrated Arabic and Sanscrit works. I have conversed both here and at home with men distinguished by their proficiency in the Eastern tongues. I am quite ready to take the Oriental learning at the valuation of the Orientalists themselves. I have never found one among them who could deny that a single shelf of a good European library was worth the whole native literature of India and Arabia. The intrinsic superiority of the Western literature is, indeed, fully admitted by those members of the Committee who support the Oriental plan of education.

It will hardly be disputed, I suppose, that the department of literature in which the Eastern writers stand highest is poetry. And I certainly never met with any Orientalist who ventured to maintain that the Arabic and Sanscrit poetry could be compared to that of the great European nations. But when we pass from works of imagination to works in which facts are recorded, and general principles investigated, the superiority of the Europeans becomes absolutely immeasurable. It is, I believe, no exaggeration to say, that all the historical information which has been collected from all the books written in the Sanscrit language is less valuable than what may be found in the most paltry abridgements used at preparatory schools in England. In every branch of physical or moral philosophy, the relative position of the two nations is nearly the same.

How, then, stands the case? We have to educate a people who cannot at present be educated by means of their mother-tongue. We must teach them some foreign language. The claims of our own language it is hardly necessary to recapitulate. It stands preeminent even among the languages of the west. It abounds with works of imagination not inferior to the noblest which Greece has bequeathed to us; with models of every species of eloquence; with historical compositions, which, considered merely as narratives, have seldom been surpassed, and which, considered as vehicles of ethical and political instruction, have never been equalled; with just and lively representations of human life and human nature; with the most profound speculations on metaphysics, morals, government, jurisprudence, and trade; with full and correct information respecting every experimental science which tends to preserve the health, to increase the comfort, or to expand the intellect of man. Whoever knows that language has ready access to all the vast intellectual wealth, which all the wisest nations of the earth have created and hoarded in the course of ninety generations. It may safely be said, that the literature now extant in that language is of far greater value than all the literature which three hundred years ago was extant in all the languages of the world together. Nor is this all. In India, English is the language

---

[6] From Thomas Babington Macaulay, "Minute of 2 February 1835 on Indian Education," *Macaulay, Prose and Poetry*, selected by G. M. Young (Cambridge MA: Harvard University Press, 1957), pp-721-24,729.

spoken by the ruling class. It is spoken by the higher class of natives at the seats of Government. It is likely to become the language of commerce throughout the seas of the East. It is the language of two great European communities which are rising, the one in the south of Africa, the other in Australasia; communities which are every year becoming more important, and more closely connected with our Indian empire. Whether we look at the intrinsic value of our literature, or at the particular situation of this country, we shall see the strongest reason to think that, of all foreign tongues, the English tongue is that which would be the most useful to our native subjects.

The question now before us is simply whether, when it is in our power to teach this language, we shall teach languages in which, by universal confession, there are no books on any subject which deserve to be compared to our own; whether, when we can teach European science, we shall teach systems which, by universal confession, whenever they differ from those of Europe, differ for the worse; and whether, when we can patronise sound Philosophy and true History, we shall countenance, at the public expense, medical doctrines, which would disgrace an English farrier [*note: a horse shoer*] -Astronomy, which would move laughter in girls at an English boarding school, History, abounding with kings thirty feet high, and reigns thirty thousand years long, and Geography, made up of seas of treacle and seas of butter.

We are not without experience to guide us. History furnishes several analogous cases, and they all teach the same lesson. There are in modem times, to go no further, two memorable instances of a great impulse given to the mind of a whole society,-of prejudices overthrown,-of knowledge diffused,-of taste purified,-of arts and sciences planted in countries which had recently been ignorant and barbarous.

The first instance to which I refer, is the great revival of letters among the Western nations at the close of the fifteenth and the beginning of the sixteenth century. At that time almost every thing that was worth reading was contained in the writings of the ancient Greeks and Romans. Had our ancestors acted as the Committee of Public Instruction has hitherto acted; had they neglected the language of Cicero and Tacitus; had they confined their attention to the old dialects of our own island; had they printed nothing and taught nothing at the universities but Chronicles in Anglo-Saxon, and Romances in Norman-French, would England have been what she now is? What the Greek and Latin were to the contemporaries of More and Ascham [*note: English humanists of the 16th century*] our tongue is to the people of India. The literature of England is now more valuable than that of classical antiquity. I doubt whether the Sanscrit literature be as valuable as that of our Saxon and Norman progenitors. In some departments,-in History, for example, I am certain that it is much less so.

In one point I fully agree with the gentlemen to whose general views I am opposed. I feel with them, that it is impossible for us, with our limited means, to attempt to educate the body of the people. We must at present do our best to form a class who may be interpreters between us and the millions whom we govern; a class of persons, Indian in blood and colour, but English in taste, in opinions, in morals, and in intellect. To that class we may leave it to refine the vernacular dialects of the country, to enrich those dialects with terms of science borrowed from the Western nomenclature, and to render them by degrees fit vehicles for conveying knowledge to the great mass of the population.

A Tryst with Destiny[7]

This speech was delivered to the Constituent Assembly of India in New Delhi on August 14 1947

Long years ago we made a tryst with destiny, and now the time comes when we shall redeem our pledge, not wholly or in full measure, but very substantially.

At the stroke of the midnight hour, when the world sleeps, India will awake to life and freedom. A moment comes, which comes but rarely in history, when we step out from the old to the new, when an age ends, and when the soul of a nation, long suppressed, finds utterance.

It is fitting that at this solemn moment we take the pledge of dedication to the service of India and her people and to the still larger cause of humanity.

At the dawn of history India started on her unending quest, and trackless centuries are filled with her striving and the grandeur of her success and her failures. Through good and ill fortune alike she has never lost sight of that quest or forgotten the ideals which gave her strength. We end today a period of ill fortune and India discovers herself again.

The achievement we celebrate today is but a step, an opening of opportunity, to the greater triumphs and achievements that await us. Are we brave enough and wise enough to grasp this opportunity and accept the challenge of the future?

Freedom and power bring responsibility. The responsibility rests upon this assembly, a sovereign body representing the sovereign people of India. Before the birth of freedom we have endured all the pains of labour and our hearts are heavy with the memory of this sorrow. Some of those pains continue even now. Nevertheless, the past is over and it is the future that beckons to us now.

That future is not one of ease or resting but of incessant striving so that we may fulfil the pledges we have so often taken and the one we shall take today. The service of India means the service of the millions who suffer. It means the ending of poverty and ignorance and disease and inequality of opportunity.

The ambition of the greatest man of our generation has been to wipe every tear from every eye. That may be beyond us, but as long as there are tears and suffering, so long our work will not be over.

And so we have to labour and to work, and work hard, to give reality to our dreams. Those dreams are for India, but they are also for the world, for all the nations and peoples are too closely knit together today for anyone of them to imagine that it can live apart.

Peace has been said to be indivisible; so is freedom, so is prosperity now, and so also is disaster in this one world that can no longer be split into isolated fragments.

To the people of India, whose representatives we are, we make an appeal to join us with faith and confidence in this great adventure. This is no time for petty and destructive criticism, no time for ill will or blaming others. We have to build the noble mansion of free India where all her children may dwell.

The appointed day has come - the day appointed by destiny - and India stands forth again, after long slumber and struggle, awake, vital, free and independent. The past clings on to us still in some measure and we have to do much before we redeem the pledges we have so often taken. Yet the turning point is past, and history begins anew for us, the history which we shall live and act and others will write about.

It is a fateful moment for us in India, for all Asia and for the world. A new star rises, the star of freedom in the east, a new hope comes into being, a vision long cherished materialises. May the star never set and that hope never be betrayed!

---

7 http://www.guardian.co.uk/theguardian/2007/may/01/greatspeeches/print

We rejoice in that freedom, even though clouds surround us, and many of our people are sorrow-stricken and difficult problems encompass us. But freedom brings responsibilities and burdens and we have to face them in the spirit of a free and disciplined people.

On this day our first thoughts go to the architect of this freedom, the father of our nation, who, embodying the old spirit of India, held aloft the torch of freedom and lighted up the darkness that surrounded us.

We have often been unworthy followers of his and have strayed from his message, but not only we but succeeding generations will remember this message and bear the imprint in their hearts of this great son of India, magnificent in his faith and strength and courage and humility. We shall never allow that torch of freedom to be blown out, however high the wind or stormy the tempest.

Our next thoughts must be of the unknown volunteers and soldiers of freedom who, without praise or reward, have served India even unto death.

We think also of our brothers and sisters who have been cut off from us by political boundaries and who unhappily cannot share at present in the freedom that has come. They are of us and will remain of us whatever may happen, and we shall be sharers in their good and ill fortune alike.

The future beckons to us. Whither do we go and what shall be our endeavour? To bring freedom and opportunity to the common man, to the peasants and workers of India; to fight and end poverty and ignorance and disease; to build up a prosperous, democratic and progressive nation, and to create social, economic and political institutions which will ensure justice and fullness of life to every man and woman.

We have hard work ahead. There is no resting for any one of us till we redeem our pledge in full, till we make all the people of India what destiny intended them to be.

We are citizens of a great country, on the verge of bold advance, and we have to live up to that high standard. All of us, to whatever religion we may belong, are equally the children of India with equal rights, privileges and obligations. We cannot encourage communalism or narrow-mindedness, for no nation can be great whose people are narrow in thought or in action.

To the nations and peoples of the world we send greetings and pledge ourselves to cooperate with them in furthering peace, freedom and democracy.

And to India, our much-loved motherland, the ancient, the eternal and the ever-new, we pay our reverent homage and we bind ourselves afresh to her service. Jai Hind [Victory to India].

Agenda – including webquest (just an example – small class)

> **Reading task "Methwold's Game" prepare - use study aids – choose 2!**
- Thursday, – web research – preparation + 2 tasks (for fiction text 2 reading to prepare) in homework
- Monday, – work in groups on topics – fiction text 2 "Rushdie's Methworld's Game" text analysis on topics
- Th., + Mo, – presentations
- We fiction text 3
- Th exam/test

- presentations start (2 per lesson, 2-4 students each)

Th.
I – Gandhi's principles (2 SuS)
I – Nehru (2 SuS)

II – India – Commonwealth (2 SuS)
II – Women (2 SuS)
II – caste system (2 SuS)

Mo.
III – Indian Press (4 SuS)
V - Bollywood (2 SuS)

Topics may differ! (literature/fiction and Englishes should be covered, if possible!)